This Book Belongs to:

_____

The Butterfly Woman

Written and Illustrated By
Colleen O'Hara-Jackson

Published by Butterflutters, Inc.
Ishpeming, Michigan

Publishing Coordination

Globe Printing, Inc. Ishpeming, Michigan

Book Layout by Stacey Willey

Edited by Roslyn McGrath

ISBN 0-9791123-0-3

ISBN 978-0-9791123-0-0

Library of Congress Control Number: 2006910028

First Printing December 2006

Other Products Available at

www.butterflutters.com

email: Wyliej1111@aol.com

Special "Thanks" to:

My mom, Nan O'Hara, "Thanks for teaching me there wasn't anything I couldn't do."

My sisters, Kathleen & Brigid, "You both have always been there for me and I so appreciate your love and support."

My brother, Tim, "Thank you for sending me the airfare for my first trip to NYC... it was life changing."

My mentor, friend and fellow "Whee" Woman, Stacey Willey ; "Without you, Butterflutters wouldn't even exist, thank you, thank you, thank you!!!!"

Maria Formolo, Sara Dean, Mary Ann Kublin, & Roslyn McGrath, "Thanks for giving me my visual inspiration for the characters in this book. Maria, you are my butterfly woman."

My "Creating Money" group, "Thanks for nurturing me to "Dream Big!"

My girlfriends - Marge, Mollie, Ms. Tracey, Roslyn, Ms. Pate, Barb, Corbin, Liz, Laurie, & Chris…the "Whee" Women in my life.

My stepdaughters, Tricia, Andrea, & Holly, "Thanks for teaching me patience and unconditional love."

My granddaughter, Alexis, "Thanks for reminding me to play, and paint often."

My nieces and nephews, Jessica, Drew, Danielle, Donovan, Dalton, Brenna, Daniel, Erin & Cavan, "Thank you for all the joy and love you've provided me in watching you grow into authentic, loving & creative people."

My mother-in-law, Stella Jackson, "Thank you for the financial support that put the wind under this project's wings."

To my husband, John, "Thank you for giving me the financial and creative freedom to fly, while teaching me to ski at the same time...brave man."

To all my friends and extended family members, especially my Unity family in Marquette, MI., "Thank you for loving me as I continue to challenge myself and grow into the second half of my life...wheeeeeeeee!!!!!!"

I love you all, Colleen

For Danielle Colleen Lawrence

"Follow your heart and your dreams will fly."

The Butterfly Woman

Written & Illustrated By:
Colleen O'Hara-Jackson

Once upon a time

… there was an old woman who lived in a small cottage on the edge of her village. Even though she was always trying to be helpful to those around her, she never felt that people truly appreciated her efforts. For years, she tried desperately to feel needed and would force her kindness on any unsuspecting soul who walked by. She was always telling those who would listen, who were very few, how to live their lives and raise

their children, even though she didn't have any children of her own. Once she even took a screaming child out of the arms of its surprised mother, who was a perfect stranger. After quieting the toddler, the old woman handed the child back to its mother thinking the woman would be pleased. Instead she told the old woman to mind her own business and stormed off. "Well!" The old woman was shocked that her efforts were not appreciated and stormed off herself!

If she wasn't helping people raise their children, she was telling them how to cook, or clean or garden. It seems the old woman knew how to do just about everything better than anyone else and was always sharing her words of wisdom whether she was asked or not. All she saw around her were struggling people who she just wanted to help in the worst way.

Every morning the old woman would cover her sagging
shoulders with a warm shawl and head to the meadow beyond
the woods with her gathering basket and shears. Once there,
she would begin to gather ripe berries for her pies and jams, and
herbs for her pickles, and wild onions for her soups and stews.

On this particular morning, as she was resting under her favorite tree, she saw the most amazing thing. A caterpillar was beginning to spin the most intriguing cocoon. The old woman was mesmerized by the dance of the caterpillar as it spun and spun and spun, enclosing itself in a perfect little home without any windows or doors. The old woman wished desperately to be able to help this little creature in any way she could, but she didn't know how.

As dusk began to fall upon the meadow, the old woman gathered her belongings and headed home, vowing to come back to check on her new-found friend in the morning.

Day after day, she returned to the same spot only to find the cocoon just hanging on the limb of the tree not doing anything. "What is happening to my little caterpillar friend?" the old woman thought to herself worriedly. Suddenly the cocoon began to move and move and move! It jerked to the left and jerked to the right and even began to twirl around and around, spinning endlessly.

Hours passed until finally the old woman could stand it no more. She grabbed her shears and cut open the cocoon.

In a blink of an eye, as if by magic, this beautiful creature peeked its head out of the slit in the cocoon. It looked around in wonder, not sure what to do next.

The old woman opened the slit wider with her hands and took the most beautiful butterfly she had ever seen from its safe haven. The butterfly sat in the palm of the old woman's hand and looked up at her with a smile. The old woman thought to herself, "Finally, someone who appreciates my help!"

The transformed caterpillar began to move its wings back and forth, testing its new found freedom as if preparing to take flight, when suddenly it lifted into the air, fluttering and fluttering. As it began to move out into the meadow, something terrible happened. The butterfly fell right out of the air and landed in the tall grass. The old woman was beside herself with worry as she scurried into the meadow looking for her fallen friend.

When she found the butterfly, it lay silent and motionless. The old woman gently picked it up into her worn and trembling hands. "What is the matter with you?" she asked the quivering little butterfly, but it was too weak to answer.

The old woman began to cry and cry and cry. She knew that the butterfly was dying and she felt somehow it was all her fault. She gently placed the butterfly back in its cocoon. She then sealed it up with some honey she had brought to have with her lunch.

After securing her small friend in its warm little home, she knelt down and began to pray. She prayed and prayed and prayed. She prayed until her knees were sore and her body ached. She prayed until the sun had fallen and the sky was filled with the Milky Way and the Moon. She prayed for an answer to why her little butterfly was so weak that it couldn't even fly to the meadow and back. She prayed asking what had gone wrong. And she prayed asking what she could do to help.

Suddenly, as if 1,000 candles had ignited all at once, a light appeared in the middle of the meadow. Out of the pulsating light appeared the most beautiful angel the old woman could ever imagine.

The speechless old woman scrambled to her feet, trembling and afraid of the angel as it began to walk towards her. Although she was scared, something deep within her assured her that she was safe and that the angel's appearance was a sign that her prayers were about to be answered.

"Who are you?" muttered the old woman as she tried to hide her wrinkled face from the splendor of the angel. "I have come to help you," the angel gently whispered in a soothing voice. "Oh, thank you!" the old woman gasped. Once again, she fell to her knees with overwhelming relief and began to cry. The angel knelt down next to the old woman and took her into her arms, rocking her back and forth…back and forth…until the old woman could cry no more.

"What happened to my beautiful friend? What went wrong?" asked the forlorn old woman. The angel cradled the old woman's face with her hands and softly replied, "The butterfly wasn't able to soar through the air because you cut open its cocoon before it was strong enough to fly. You see, my dear, the butterfly needs to struggle inside the cocoon. It needs to push back and forth and to and fro in order to build strength in its wings, so they can carry it into the wind. I know you thought by making an opening in its cocoon you were helping, but really you kept it from gaining the strength it needed to take flight."

The old woman was racked with guilt and shame because suddenly she understood why people didn't appreciate her efforts. All these years she had assumed she was helping when really she was hindering people from being strong and independent. With this knowledge, she began once again to sob in the arms of the angel.

"Shhh…it's going to be all right," the angel assured her. "How can they ever forgive me?" whimpered the old woman. Holding her shoulders, the angel looked straight into the old woman's eyes and said, "You must first forgive yourself. Once you have cleansed yourself of the guilt and shame, you will have opened the door for others to follow. Forgiveness is a simple act of love, my friend, but not always easy." As the old woman drank in the blueness of the eyes that stared back at her, a sense of peace washed over her like a gentle spring rain. The angel took the old woman in her arms and rocked her until she had fallen into a deep and restful sleep.

The old woman awoke as the sun began to warm her face and the smell of fresh dew embraced her nostrils. She opened her eyes realizing she had spent the night underneath the tree where the cocoon hung on the branch above her. She sat up with a start, suddenly remembering the episode with the butterfly and the angel. She looked around half expecting the angel to still be there, but seeing no one, her attention once again focused on the silent cocoon. As she stood up and faced the burden of guilt and shame of what she had done, she thought she saw it move, if only so slightly. "Could it be? Is it possible my prayers really were answered? No. It was probably just my imagination getting the best of me," she thought to herself as she continued to gaze upon the cocoon hanging in front of her. Suddenly, the cocoon **did** move and she knew she wasn't imagining it. It not only moved to the right, but then it moved to the left. "Oh, my! Oh, my! Could this really be happening? Can this really be true?" the old woman shouted with glee.

As the cocoon began the dance of life, the old woman danced right along with it. She danced for the butterfly. She danced for the angel. She danced for all the people she thought she had helped over the years. She danced for joy and forgiveness and for love. But, most importantly, she danced for herself. She danced for the courage at her age to change and to learn and to grow.

And while she was dancing, a miracle emerged before her eyes. With a burst of color, the butterfly who only hours ago was weak and dying, shot out of its cocoon with such joy, the old woman began a giggle that soon turned into laughter that sprang from the depths of her soul. Together the old woman and the beautiful butterfly danced among the flowers of the welcoming meadow.

From that day forward the old woman became a true friend to all who crossed her path. She never again assumed that people she thought were struggling needed her help, but always offered a helping hand. And all those who accepted her kindness knew that it had been given from the heart, and that their lives had been touched with the wings of love.

The End

About the Author

Colleen O'Hara-Jackson graduated from Eastern Michigan University with a BS Degree in Theatre, and a minor in Art. An award-winning actress, as well as an accomplished writer, director and theatre producer, Colleen has found great joy in venturing off into a new direction and creating her first book. She currently lives with her husband, John, in God's country, the Upper Peninsula of Michigan.

www.butterflutters.com donates 10% of all profits to people and/or organizations that support creative freedom and growth.

Butterflutters
Original Art & Poetry by Colleen O'Hara-Jackson

The "Whee" Women Series
Sample Card

"The Sea Goddess"

"She swims
In the
Deep recesses
Of our Hearts'
Dreams.
Where
A Never
Ending
Wave
Of Desire
Washes over
Our imaginations,
And
Creates
The
Souls'
Paradise."

"Unity"

"A Circle of Light & Love.
An unbroken
Ring of color
Surrounding the spectrum
Of
Universal Truth.
It's core.
A rainbow,
A coalition connected.
One Heart.
One Mind.
One Being.
One."

The Butterfly Series
Sample Card

Black & White Series
Sample Card

Playfulness

"I am playfulness,
My curiosity
Allows me the freedom
To experience life,
With the "heart" of a child.
Come and explore
With me, won't you?
I know our friendship
Has the power to spread
Joy, Laughter & Love,
Throughout the
World.
Are you ready
For an adventure?
I Am!"

View all designs at www.Butterflutters.com